Everything
You Need to
Know About

Weapons in School and at Home

After a shooting at Jefferson High School in New York City, police set up barricades and reinforced security.

Everything You Need to Know About Weapons in School and at Home

Jay Schleifer

The Rosen Publishing Group, Inc.
New York

Published in 1994, 2000 by The Rosen Publishing Group, Inc.
29 East 21st Street, New York, NY 10010

Library of Congress Cataloging-in-Publication Data

Schleifer, Jay
    Everything you need to know about weapons in school and at home / Jay Schleifer. — rev. ed.
        p.   cm. — (The Need to know library)
    Includes bibliographical references and index.
    ISBN 0-8239-3315-6
    1. Gun control—United States 2. Firearms ownership—United States. 3. School violence—United States. 4. Firearms—Safety measures. 5. Weapons—Safety measures. I. Title. II. Title: Weapons in school and at home. III. Series.
HV436.S35 1994
363.3'3'0973—dc20
                                      93-41940
                                          CIP
                                          AC

Manufactured in the United States of America

Contents

Introduction: Note from the Author

Dear Reader:

It may seem unusual to begin a book like this with a personal story from the author's family, but I think you'll see why we have chosen to do so. The story in chapter 1 is about a young woman named Laura. Laura is my daughter. At the time, she was going to a junior high school probably a lot like yours.

Hopefully, what happened to her at that school will never happen to you.

Here's the story, told by Laura herself. Most of the names and dates have been changed. The rest of the story is frighteningly true.

Jay Schleifer

Chapter One | A Lesson in Violence: A True Story

*J*anuary 12 was cloudy and a little chilly, but nothing unusual for winter in New England. It was just a regular day in the seventh grade at our junior high school—or so I thought.

Then something bizarre happened—right in the middle of sixth-period English class—that turned this ordinary day into the most frightening experience of my life.

I remember it clearly, even though it happened years ago. Our teacher had just handed back the quizzes we'd taken the day before, when suddenly the classroom door flew open.

There stood Charlie C., well known as the "bad boy" of the eighth grade. Only today he wasn't lugging his usual giant boom box around. Instead, he had what looked like a plastic toy gun slung over his right shoulder.

What was going on? Why was Charlie fooling around? Charlie's gun couldn't be real, could it? Things like that didn't happen in our small, quiet town. Weapons were found only in big city schools, right?

Wrong. We soon learned that the gun was real. That morning Charlie had been suspended by the principal, Mr. Davis, for refusing to take his hat off in the building. Charlie vowed he'd come back and kill the principal.

Mr. Davis had been a school official for many years. In that time, he'd heard threats from a lot of angry kids. But this one was for real. When Charlie got home, he broke into his grandfather's gun collection, took out one of the guns, loaded it, and started back to school.

When Charlie returned, he headed straight for the main office. His first shot went through a hallway window, missing Mr. Davis but hitting a secretary in the arm. Mr. Davis was cut by flying glass.

Bill, the janitor, happened to be in that part of the building at the time of the shooting. The young father of two was well liked. Bill asked Charlie what he was doing. When Charlie refused to answer, Bill said, "I'll have to call the police."

Cornered, frightened, and half-crazy, Charlie pulled the trigger several times. Bill died at Charlie's feet, in a pool of blood on the floor he'd

Many innocent bystanders have been victims of gunfire in the streets and in schools.

polished only hours before.

Now Charlie, a murderer at age thirteen, stood at our classroom door. He was looking for a way out. He tried grabbing the teacher as a hostage. Just then a boy near the door jumped from his seat, yelling, "Take me! Take me!"

At first the boy thought it was all a big joke. He went on laughing as Charlie paraded him in the hallway. But soon we heard sirens and a loud voice over the P.A. system ordering Charlie to drop the gun. The boy began to cry. It was no joke.

The teacher screamed for all of us to crouch behind her desk in the corner of the room. As we huddled there, I looked at my classmates. Some were sobbing, some were too stunned to cry.

During the next two hours, Charlie roamed the hall and classrooms like an animal on the loose.

The police tried everything to persuade Charlie to give himself up. They finally found Charlie's aunt and rushed her to school. She pleaded with Charlie over the P.A. system.

"I can't!" Charlie screamed back. "Don't you see that I can't!" After what seemed like forever, Charlie caved in. He shoved the boy clear. Then he walked to the window and tossed the gun out.

Officers charged in immediately, jumped Charlie, and pinned him to the floor. One officer shoved a gun to the side of his head as others handcuffed him. It was over. Meanwhile, the vice principal, not knowing if there were other shooters, started screaming, "Get out! Get out of the building!"

We ran down the empty halls and headed outside—right into 200 cops pointing loaded guns at us. Practically every news reporter in the state was there.

That night, all three major TV networks reported the story about our school. By morning, we were on almost every front page in the nation. It was the most fame the school, or the town, had ever had. But it wasn't the kind of fame anyone wanted. School was closed the next day for Bill's funeral. The day after that was spent talking in class about all that had happened.

In time, things settled down. Charlie was locked up in the toughest part of the state juvenile center. They'll hold him there as long as the law allows.

The principal retired not long after the incident. My teacher, who was sort of a hero, still gives English quizzes in the same room. And the kid who was taken hostage went on to graduate with honors.

For me, nothing was ever quite the same. It's one thing to read about guns in someone else's school. It's another to have your own young life in the hands of an out-of-control teenager. But unlike Bill, at least I did live through it.

Laura Schleifer

According to a recent study, almost 8 percent of high school students reported carrying a gun to school for protection.

Chapter Two

A World of Weapons

The gun that Charlie C. brought to school that day was an example of a growing problem in America: weapons in the hands of young people. A recent survey by the U.S. Centers for Disease Control (CDC) revealed that more than 30 percent of high school students reported carrying a weapon at least once in the past month.

For the survey, the CDC defined a weapon as a knife, razor, club, or gun. But almost anything can be used as a weapon, even if it was not made for that purpose—bricks, bottles, baseball bats, box cutters, and even someone's hands or feet. But it's the items that are designed to be used against another person or living thing—such as switchblade knives, "Oriental fighting sticks," and, of course, guns—that cause the most damage.

In the United States, homicide is the second leading

cause of death among teens ages thirteen to nineteen. And the weapon most commonly used in such homicides is a gun. The rate of violent death among teens, especially by gunfire, is growing. Between 1985 and 1995, the number of juveniles murdered by firearms rose by 153 percent in the United States. Almost 8 percent of high school students surveyed by the CDC reported carrying a gun to school for protection or self-defense.

An Epidemic of Violence

Despite such sensational and horrifying incidents as the mass murders committed in recent years by teens at their schools in places such as Littleton, Colorado; Springfield, Oregon; Paducah, Kentucky; and Pearl, Mississippi; the rate of violence by teens actually slowed somewhat in the last years of the twentieth century. Despite this decline, Mark Rosenberg of the CDC says the problem is far from solved. According to Rosenberg, teen violence has become a kind of epidemic. "I don't think any country not at war has ever had to deal with this problem," Rosenberg says. "New forms of youth violence, like an infectious disease, keep emerging."

On average, more than 30,000 Americans die each year as a result of gunfire. Teens make up a large part of that group. In fact, in the 1990s the rate of death by gunfire rose faster among teens than any other age group.

In the last decade, the firearm-related homicide rate in the United States was almost sixteen times higher than in all the other industrialized countries of the world combined! The firearm-related suicide rate was nearly eleven times higher, and the accidental firearm-related death rate was nine times higher.

According to the Violence Policy Center, at the current pace, firearm-related deaths will surpass automobile accidents as the leading cause of death among young Americans in the first decade of the twenty-first century. In fact, it already has in certain parts of the country, such as New York, California, Texas, and the District of Columbia.

Guns are only part of the problem. Other kinds of weapons are harder to keep track of. But for every gun attack, there are said to be about five knife attacks.

You may be asking yourself why society hasn't banded together to rid itself of all weapons and the threat they represent. To understand, you need to look more closely at the special place weapons, especially guns, have in American society.

"Make My Day!"

We live in a world of weapons. You don't need to look very far to see how widespread and accepted they are.

Start by turning on your television. Incidents involving weapons are sure to be on the news. Many times these stories are discussed even before important world events.

Or perhaps you tune in to any number of action shows or movies about crime and the police. An example of such movies comes from superstar Clint Eastwood's successful "Dirty Harry" series. In it, Eastwood, playing a tough police hero, stares down the sight of a powerful gun he's pointing at the bad guy and says the now-famous words, "Go ahead, make my day!"

The next time you walk through a toy store, head for the "Action Toys" department. You'll probably find an assortment of toy guns and rifles, bows and arrows, plastic swords, knives, grenades, and space weapons.

There's really nothing new about all this. In America, weapons have always been an important part of life and somewhat glorified in children's play. Native Americans used the bow and arrow, spear, and lance to hunt and to protect themselves. They celebrated their weapons in traditional dances and decorated art.

The first European settlers brought guns with them to America. Later, settlers used their guns to fight the British in the Revolutionary War. Then people moved westward. Anyone who has ever seen a cowboy movie knows something about the Wild West. It is shown as a place where most males had a six-shooter hanging from their belt or a rifle in their saddlebag. That's probably stretching the truth a bit. But even the famous gun-maker, Colt Firearms, calls its .45 caliber revolver "the Gun That Won the West."

Weapons in Other Nations

Other nations have a tradition of using weapons, too.

Weapons and violence are often glorified in American culture.

But it's more a matter of honoring their military forces than arming their private citizens. The British, for example, don't normally arm their police officers. Instead, British "bobbies" patrol their beat with only a nightstick for protection. Amazing as it may seem, British criminals seem to play by the same rules. For the most part, they do not use guns in their crimes.

The nations of the Far East invented both the martial arts, such as karate and kung fu, and unusual weapons, such as fighting stars and sticks. Many martial arts movies show the training and the discipline necessary to master these ways of fighting, but they fail to explain the rules and philosophy behind many of the martial arts. They do not make it clear that for many, this kind of violence is used only for self-defense. It is considered the last step to be taken when there is no other way to solve matters peacefully.

But things may be changing in other nations as well. Weapons violence seems to be on the rise. Some people blame U.S. TV shows and movies. As this kind of entertainment gains popularity worldwide, critics fear that weapons violence may increase along with it.

Is Seeing Believing?

It has been estimated that the typical child in the United States "witnesses" more than 200,000 acts of violence, including 25,000 murders, in the mass media—television, films, popular music, magazines and newspapers, video games, the Internet—by the time he or she is eighteen. Fifteen-year-old Kipland Kinkel, who murdered his parents and several schoolmates in Springfield, Oregon, in 1998, attributed his troubled state of mind to "role-playing games, heavy-metal music, violent cartoons/TV, and sugared cereal." According to Barry Kristberg, president of the National Council on Crime and Delinquency, "The violence in the media and the easy availability of guns are what's driving the slaughter of the innocents."

Others say that most young people can easily tell the difference between what's real and what's make-believe. They remind us that millions of television watchers grow up normally without being troubled or influenced by the violence they see. But nobody really knows the long-term effects of viewing so much violence. It's scary to think that acts of violence on television may cause the very same acts to happen in real life.

This, however, is fact: The "tools of violence" are all around today's youngsters. According to the most recent comprehensive survey, conducted by the National Institute of Justice (NIJ), the research arm of the U.S. Department of Justice, some 44 million Americans own firearms. That accounts for a total of 192 million firearms, 65 million of which are handguns. Gun ownership is heavily concentrated. Although only 25 percent of American adults and 35 percent of households in the United States own guns, 74 percent of gun owners own two or more.

Some students feel that they need to carry a gun for self-protection.

In addition, Worldwatch Institute reports that half of the world's 500 million small arms—defined as grenades, land mines, and, most important, military-style assault rifles—are in circulation in the United States. According to Daniel Gross, founder of the anti-gun violence group PAX, these statistics explain a lot about the rise in teen violence. "The reality is, these tragedies make a lot of sense," Gross believes. "Everybody wonders, How do kids get this way? How does something like this happen? I'll tell you exactly how: The kids had access to guns."

Taking a Chance

Many people agree that guns in themselves are not bad.

Most guns in private hands are meant for hunting or sports shooting, not hurting people. Some are in private collections. And other weapons are kept by their owners for protection against crime. The vast majority of weapons never cause a problem.

But where there's a weapon, there's always the chance that it may get into the wrong hands and be used for the wrong purpose. That means there's always a need for the owner of that weapon to take extra precautions to make sure this doesn't happen.

Many people believe that every citizen has a right to own a gun either for hunting or self-defense.

Chapter Three | The Right to Bear Arms

Because weapons are so much a part of life, they can be legally owned in most nations. In fact, the United States even has a major law that protects a private citizen's right to own a gun.

The law, which dates back to 1791, is found in the Second Amendment of the U.S. Constitution and is often known as "the Right to Bear Arms." It's part of the Bill of Rights, the same list of laws that grants Americans freedom of speech and religion. The law says that citizens should always have the right to keep guns so they'll always be able to defend their freedom.

It's pretty clear why the law was passed when it was. The Americans had just used weapons to gain their independence from England. They had fought the British in the Revolutionary War and wanted to secure their future.

But that's not all the law says. It also says these guns

should be kept because the nation needs to have a "militia." A militia means a part-time army of citizens, like the National Guard, called upon for service in times of emergency. Such organizations keep their guns locked up in a central place.

Some Americans believe that lawmakers in the 1700s did not mean for private citizens to own guns when they weren't serving in the militia. Others believe that the lawmakers did intend for private citizens to keep arms and to take their guns with them to serve in the militia. What did the Founding Fathers mean? They can't tell us. They've been dead for over 100 years!

The Great Gun-Control Debate

The issue is gun control, and the following arguments present the pros and cons of the debate.

Pro

Those who are for gun control favor the banning of privately owned guns. They believe the result will be a huge drop in violence and the saving of many lives. Not only would accidents be prevented if there were no legally owned guns but it would be harder for criminals to get hold of guns. If there are fewer guns in public hands, there are fewer guns to steal. All of society would benefit. Gun-control advocates believe that the enormous cost of police, medical, and social services needed to deal with gun-related problems would drop sharply.

Con

Those who are against gun control favor private ownership of guns. They often point out that "guns don't kill, people do." They see violent people as the real problem. And they claim that if there were no guns in the hands of the public, such dangerous people would find other weapons.

What's more, gun-owner groups feel that banning guns would have no effect on criminal use. Criminals own guns now! They won't change their ways just because the laws change. These groups point out that if legally owned guns were banned, only the criminals would have weapons. Lawful citizens would be unprotected.

The gun-owner groups think that the answer to the problem of accidents with weapons lies in better training and safety. They ask why gun owners who practice weapons safety should be made to suffer because other gun owners are careless.

The Law Stands

There are powerful organizations on each side, spending millions of dollars to convince lawmakers and the public that their view is the right one.

But whenever gun-control laws have been put forward, the courts have allowed the Right to Bear Arms to stand. Private gun ownership is legal under certain conditions—one of which directly affects young people.

Limits to the Law

Here are some of the conditions for private ownership of guns, both in the United States and elsewhere:

- ◆ No one under eighteen can legally own a handgun of any kind.

- ◆ It is illegal to privately own automatic weapons, or assault-style weapons, without a special permit. Such firearms are designed to fire a steady stream of bullets. However, a huge number of such weapons are in circulation in the United States illegally, and many legal firearms can be easily modified to have assault capabilities.

- ◆ A person with a serious criminal record or record of mental illness can't legally own a firearm. By law, a person seeking to buy weapons almost always has to undergo a background check.

- ◆ Some local areas have other special laws, often about carrying concealed weapons. These are weapons that are hidden from view. Schools and businesses have the right to make their own rules about banning weapons.

- ◆ In other nations, such as Canada, Great Britain, and Japan, there is no built-in right to own guns. A private owner needs a permit to own one. To get a gun permit, a person needs a valid reason, such as a job as a bank guard.

Gun control continues to be the subject of heated debate in America.

Can All Weapons Be Banned?

When it comes to other weapons, such as knives, the law is less clear. The problem is that many items that are used as weapons were intended for regular, non-harmful, everyday use. A knife, for example, has many practical, everyday uses—as a kitchen utensil, for example—that harm no one. A brick can be used as a weapon in an assault, but its primary use is as a building material. It is difficult, if not impossible, to legislate against possession of such common items as axes, bats, hammers, and box cutters, all of which are designed for legitimate use but are also often used in committing crimes. In contrast, a switchblade knife has few legitimate uses other than as a weapon.

The law usually works by making the penalty greater if someone uses a weapon in a crime than if no weapon is used. Armed robbery can result in more jail time than simple robbery. Assault (attack on a person) with a deadly weapon is a far more serious crime than simple assault. And that's even if the weapon used turns out to be a common kitchen knife, ice pick, or bicycle chain.

It seems likely that there will always be weapons around young people. More laws cannot guarantee public safety. What can the owners of those weapons, other adults, and young people do to keep kids from dying or getting hurt? Ask yourself what you can do in your own neighborhood.

Chapter Four

Weapons in the Home

*P*ete was furious. Final grades were out, and his were not good. The coach benched him just before the big game. His dad got mad and grounded him for the rest of the semester. Now Pete wouldn't even see the big game. Gloria, his girlfriend, would be there—maybe with somebody else.

Pete decided he'd make them all suffer. His dad's gun cabinet was never locked, so he pulled a weapon out and loaded it. For a long time, Pete sat and looked at the sleek, black-barreled gun. Then he sat down and wrote a short note. Finally, he put the gun to his head and pulled the trigger.

Terri and Paul had been married just a year, but the honeymoon was clearly over. They fought all the time, usually over money or their families. Most of their friends felt that the marriage would

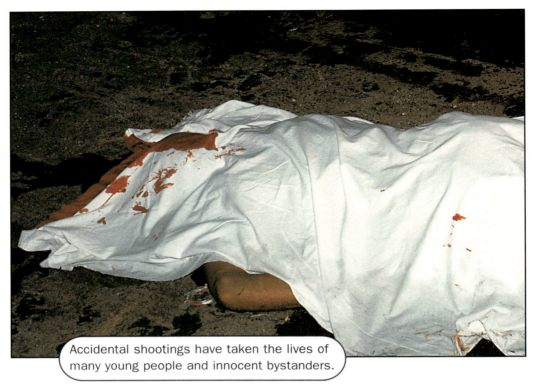

Accidental shootings have taken the lives of many young people and innocent bystanders.

rooms for accidental shootings. Every other day in the United States, a child dies from an accident involving a gun. Each day, 1.2 million American children arrive home from school to a house or apartment in which there is a gun but no parent present.

Accidents

The army term "smart weapons" doesn't always apply to the weapons people have in their homes. Nor does the word "smart" apply to some of their owners!

Guns are often left out in the open. Even with small children around, many gun owners leave their weapons in convenient spots. Sometimes the owner shows a child exactly where he or she is putting a gun, then says, "Don't ever open this drawer and touch this." These words, of course, make the youngster curious. As soon as the adult is away, the youngster heads for the forbidden drawer.

Weapons are left loaded. Some people want to be prepared for the unexpected. Parents may think they are being careful by removing the cartridge clip (bullet-storage unit). But many people forget to remove the ready-to-fire round already in the gun's firing chamber. Thinking the weapon is unloaded, people who pick it up are not always careful handling it.

Acting out of fear. An untrained person who buys a gun for protection may react to sights and sounds too quickly. He or she may think there is a prowler and fire at the wrong target. This happens more often than most people think. In one study, only about 15 percent of the shots were directed at the intended targets.

What do you call harmless? Many people consider air rifles, sometimes called BB guns, as harmless toys. Adults buy them for children or teens to use in target shooting or for hunting small animals. Often there are no laws to control who buys and uses them.

At one time, air rifles were fairly low-powered. The rifle would be dangerous only to the eye or other delicate areas. But in recent years, air-rifle manufacturers have come out with more powerful models. Prospective gun owners may be unaware that some newer model rifles have a punch close to that of a .38 caliber handgun, the same size that police carry.

Air rifles can be serious weapons! They should be

handled with caution by responsible adults and by youngsters who are supervised by responsible adults. They should never be pointed at another person.

Did You Know?

The debate continues as to whether having a gun in the home adds to a family's safety. Those who argue for gun ownership argue that no statistics can prove or disprove their case, since there is no way to demonstrate, with numbers, how many crimes are deterred by the idea that a gun may be present in a home or household. However, there seems to be little doubt that a gun in the home is an increased safety risk. Consider:

- ◆ On average, more than 1,200 Americans are killed each year in unintentional shootings, most of which take place in the home. That's more than three deaths each day.

- ◆ It is estimated that for every time a gun is used to successfully defend a home against a criminal or intruder, there are 1.3 accidental deaths, 4.6 criminal homicides, and 37 suicides using firearms.

- ◆ According to the Violence Policy Center, a public policy study group, having a gun in the home makes it three times more likely that you, a family member, or a close friend will be murdered by a family member or intimate partner.

- Studies indicate that in a majority of cases where a child shoots another child, the shooter is another family member, usually a sibling, most often a brother. In a significant percentage of those cases, the child does not know that the gun is loaded.

- In an average year, only 1 percent of actual or attempted victims of crime use a firearm to defend themselves. Almost six times as many Americans each year have a gun they own stolen from them.

- Historically, the homicide rate in the United States has been highest in those regions of the country where gun ownership is highest and the least strictly regulated.

Suicides

Having a gun in the home also greatly increases the risk that a seriously depressed or troubled family member will succeed in a suicide attempt. That risk is even greater for teens and young adults in such situations. In the last half of the twentieth century, the suicide rate among young adults more than tripled. In the last two decades, 80 percent of that increase came from suicides committed with a gun. Simultaneously, suicide using other methods declined. A recent study in the prestigious *New England Journal of Medicine* suggests that the presence of one or more guns in the home increases the risk of suicide in that home by almost five times.

Doctors know that many times the urge to take one's life is impulsive. It may be a sudden reaction to something that has happened. When these strong feelings come up, if there's no easy way to commit suicide, there's a chance that the urge might pass. If a person does try suicide by some other means, such as taking too many pills, doctors might have a better chance of saving the person's life. The quick and massive wound made by a bullet is usually fatal.

Fights and Family Violence

There is one more important way in which having a gun in the home may make that home a less safe place in which to live. Just as the presence of a gun in the home makes it more likely that a seriously depressed person will use a weapon in a suicide attempt, the presence of a gun in the home makes it more likely that a gun will be used in a domestic dispute.

This is not, of course, the same as saying that gun owners are necessarily more violent than those who do not own guns. All families argue, over big and small matters. Whether or not the matter at issue seems trivial to an outsider, family arguments often are very passionate and can quickly become heated, even violent.

But one thing is certain: If there are no guns in the

home, a family quarrel is not going to be settled by gun-fire. Though such quarrels may still lead to violence, in the absence of a gun that violence is much less likely to end in death. Statistics show that having a gun in the home more than triples the likelihood that a family member will be murdered by another family member or sexual partner. The use of a gun in a domestic violence situation makes it more than twelve times more likely that the disagreement will end in a death.

These risks are even greater for women. The presence of a gun in the home makes the risk of suicide among women in that home almost five times greater and the risk of homicide at the hands of a family member or sexual partner nearly three times greater.

Some Final Thoughts

There are valid reasons to have weapons at home. It is also true that a large number of weapons in homes seldom cause problems. There are ways home-owners can reduce the risks associated with weapons.

Still, the possibility of accidents and family violence (even suicides) are more real when weapons are available. It is important to know the facts about gun safety and to understand the responsibilities involved. It may help to decide if owning a weapon is right for your family.

Chapter Five

Dangers in the Classroom

The headlines were everywhere, terrifying and unavoidable. It was as if, in the last few years of the twentieth century, the increase in violence among the nation's young people—at home, on the streets, and in school—had reached an unspeakable climax.

Earlier in the 1990s, much of the talk about the so-called epidemic of violence among the nation's teens had focused on gang-related activities, often associated with the use and sale of drugs, particularly cocaine. Rightly or wrongly, many Americans regarded this rise in violence, and the increased use of weapons by America's youth, as an urban problem—that is, a problem confined mainly to the nation's largest cities. Likewise, many Americans believed that the growing problem with weapons and violence was of chief concern among poor people and members of minority groups. The stereotypical image of youth violence in the nation was a young African-American male from a big city—a "gangbanger," dressed in hip-hop garb and his gang's colors, in the company of his posse, on the mean streets of the roughest section of one of the country's scariest cities, where only the most unfortunate and disreputable members of society lived. For most people, such violence happened "somewhere else," far away from where "good, normal" people lived.

But in the last three years of the twentieth century, the face of youth violence has changed. Now it resembles baby-faced Andrew Golden, age eleven, and his friend Mitchell Johnson, thirteen, of Jonesboro, Arkansas, who shot at fifteen of their schoolmates, killing five, after pulling a fire alarm to lure their victims outside the school. It looks like undersized, high-spirited Kipland Kinkel, age fifteen, who murdered his parents and then shot twenty-six of his classmates, killing four, in Springfield, Oregon. It looks like pudgy, confused Luke Woodham, age fifteen, who opened fire at fellow students at his high school in Pearl, Mississippi, leaving two of them dead. And it looks like bookish Michael Carneal, fourteen, who took aim at a prayer group in his high school in West Paducah, Kentucky, killing three and injuring five.

Finally, perhaps most indelibly, it looks like Eric Harris and Dylan Klebold, seniors at Columbine High School in Littleton, Colorado. Harris and Klebold shot a dozen of their schoolmates to death and wounded more than

On April 20, 1999, in the deadliest school shooting yet, Dylan Klebold and Eric Harris killed twelve and injured more than twenty at Columbine High School.

twenty. Though their plans to demolish the school with explosives failed, they succeeded in making Columbine a shorthand term for a new kind of random, mass violence that threatens the nation's schools.

Not Just Cities, Not Just High Schools

In one way, the school shooters shared something in common with the prevailing stereotype of the violent teen criminal: They were all male. In other important ways, however, they were quite different. First, all of them were white. All were from two-parent families that were seen by friends, teachers, and neighbors as "normal" and even "successful." None was involved with drugs or gangs. All were from rural or suburban schools and towns, the kinds of places that people move to in order to escape "big city problems" like violence and crime, the kinds of places where, it was thought, there was no need for metal detectors in schools to check for weapons. All of the attackers shot their victims at random. Virtually all of them grew up in families that kept guns in the home, in parts of the country where hunting, self-defense, and gun ownership were an accepted part of the culture. Virtually all had been given their first guns or been taught to shoot by parents or family members. As a seventh-grader at Westside School in Jonesboro explained, no one thought it was unusual that a thirteen-year-old like Mitchell

Johnson had access to a gun because "everybody at Westside knows how to shoot a gun." Virtually all of the school shooters assembled their arsenals by taking guns from their own homes or their neighbors' homes.

So what do the school shootings tell us? They tell us that the issue of weapons at home and in school is not just an urban problem, not just a minority problem, not just a problem of poverty, but a national problem that needs to be addressed in every sector of society. A familiarity with weapons, and their easy availability, makes it that much more likely that a troubled teen will use a weapon to "resolve" his or her conflicts. As Frank Sanchez, the director of delinquency prevention for the Boys and Girls Clubs of America, points out, "The latest cases reveal that youth violence transcends economic status and ethnicity. No longer are the inner cities and urban settings of America alone vulnerable to this kind of random violence." In short, it can happen anywhere.

Easy-to-Get Weapons

In the United States, no one under eighteen can legally own a handgun. (So-called long guns, such as rifles and shotguns, are much less strictly regulated.) But with almost 200 million privately owned firearms in the United States, guns can be very easy to obtain, even for teens.

ABC News wanted to see for itself how available guns were in school. They put some young-looking

In the United States, guns are plentiful and easy to get, even for teens.

undercover reporters in a typical school. Even though these "students" were new to the school, they were able to buy handguns from other students within one day. In fact, they had a choice of weapons, at different prices.

In another area, a reporter for *Newsweek* magazine asked local teens how easy it was to find guns in the neighborhood. "Easier to find than a copy of *Newsweek*," a teen told him.

Where do all these weapons come from? Some are stolen, but studies show that a large percentage of the guns in school belong to parents or other adults in the family. They are simply brought from home.

Why do so many teens today feel they need to carry weapons? Experts in teen behavior give these answers.

A Pocketful of Power

All young people like to be admired for being in control. They also like to have others take them seriously. Unfortunately, many youngsters don't believe in their own abilities. They try to get admiration and respect by carrying weapons. One young man put it this way: "When I had a gun or a knife, nobody could touch me."

Sadly, the young man made this statement at a state prison, where he's currently serving a life term for shooting a school official.

All the Kids Do It!

Teens are naturals at playing "follow the leader." They are often strongly influenced by peer pressure. But most of the fads they copy from their friends, like wearing baseball caps backward or torn jeans, are harmless. Carrying weapons, on the other hand, is not. Still, some kids carry weapons just because their friends do.

Gang members often have to carry weapons as a condition of membership. It's part of the gang rules. It's also a way to keep gang members from going to the police. "Before you tell the police about our illegal weapons," warn the gang leaders, "remember that you carry, too."

Sometimes little children pack a gun or a knife so they can be like a big sister or brother. They may not be aware of the danger. It's sad to think that they look up to the very siblings who can get them killed.

The Answer to Life's Problems

Some experts who study juvenile behavior say that society has taught young people to use violence to solve problems. Every time the star in an action movie "blows away" the bad guys and walks off a hero, or the bad guys are cheered by their friends and escape police action, that lesson is reinforced.

Self-Defense

Perhaps the most tragic reason that some young people carry weapons is self-defense. Isn't it time for society to take action when a young person feels the need to defend him- or herself from a weapon carried by another kid? Protection was the reason one fifteen-year-old gave for having a powerful .357 Magnum pistol in his bookbag. He never imagined that the gun would go off as he reached inside. But a shot did fire. It went right through the chest of one student nearby and killed a second person.

Today's schools are facing weapons problems like never before. But there is hope. Many parents and concerned citizens are working hard to come up with some solutions. You'll read about some of their ideas in the next chapter.

James Brady and his wife, Sarah, applaud the passing of the Brady Bill, which promotes stronger gun restrictions.

Chapter Six

Calling for an End to Weapons Violence

Most parents and adults love children. They hate—and will find ways to fight—anything that seriously threatens the young.

Weapons violence at home and in school is exactly that kind of threat. Here are some steps parents, teachers, police, and other adults—with the help of young people—have begun to take.

Crack Down!

As you walk into certain Chicago schools, you'll find yourself walking into Operation SAFE (Schools Are For Education). It's an antiweapons program put together by the Chicago school system.

The heart of the program is a set of portable metal detectors. Chicago School Safety Director George Sams tells why portables are used: "A lot of schools want to put detectors in every school and use them every day. It won't work. If kids know they have to pass through a detector and that the detector will always be in the same place, they'll get the guns in through windows or back doors."

Instead, Sams's detectors are always on the move, popping up where least expected. So far, the program seems to be working.

Another key part of the SAFE program is a linkup between city police and school building guards. Under the law, police officers can't search a person unless they have a good reason to believe he or she is a lawbreaker.

School guards work under a looser set of rules. They can search a student just because they have a hunch he or she might be up to something. But they lack a police officer's power to make an arrest.

Under the linkup, the guards use their search power to stop and search young people as police stand by and watch. If a weapon is found, the police officer is right there to make an arrest.

In other "get tough" programs, parents are arrested if a child gets hold of a gun they own and is hurt or uses the weapon in a crime. The parents can go to jail, even though they took no active part in a crime!

Gun-owners' groups think that laws that hold parents responsible for their children's involvement with guns are unfair. "A child is five times as likely to drown as to be hurt with a firearm," they argue. "Yet no one is

More young people and women are attending classes in gun safety than ever before.

making laws against pool owners." But regardless of the protest, the laws have gone into effect.

Perhaps the toughest action of all is that more states have passed laws allowing them to try teens who commit crimes with a weapon as adults rather than as juveniles. (In legal terms, a juvenile is a person who is younger than legal age, which is eighteen in most states. A juvenile generally enjoys different legal rights and protections than does an adult.) Twenty-seven states currently allow a juvenile who commits a crime to be prosecuted as an adult. The rest have a minimum age at which a juvenile can be tried as an adult. A juvenile who is tried as an adult can be sentenced to the same punishment that an adult would receive, including the death penalty.

Currently, there are more than seventy people awaiting execution on death row in the nation's prisons for crimes they committed while not yet legally adults. Since 1990, the United States is one of only six countries in the world that has legally executed juveniles. (The others are Saudi Arabia, Yemen, Iran, Pakistan, and Nigeria.)

Get Smart!

Gun-owners' groups have their own programs, which often focus on weapons safety. The largest such group is the National Rifle Association (NRA). The NRA puts on a program for elementary school children called "Eddie Eagle." The program uses coloring books to teach children to stay clear of any firearm they come across. More than 1.5 million youngsters, in some 3,000 schools, have had this program made available to them.

Another program, called STAR (Straight Talk About Risks), is run by a group called the Center to Prevent Handgun Violence, a group in favor of gun control. STAR has created activities and materials aimed at four grade levels. The youngest group (kindergarten through second grade) gets comic books that describe the battle between two imaginary groups, the Yooks and the Zooks. The battle is over which side of the bread should be buttered.

Although this story may seem ridiculous, its real aim is to teach young kids how to handle the angry feelings that lead to violence. One program also talks about weapons used in violent acts and understanding the difference between real and make-believe violence.

In high school, STAR students put on plays and do projects involving weapons and violence. The activities are more mature, but the learning goals are the same.

Get Involved!

In some communities, concerned parents have taken an active part in dealing with weapons violence in schools. They have formed Safety Watch programs in which parent squads patrol school hallways. Local businesses take part, too. They donate money or allow parents to take time off from work with pay in order to participate in school patrols.

There's even a special educational group set up to research and deal with school violence and weapons problems. The National School Safety Council (NSSC) carries out studies, puts out newsletters and magazines, and offers teachers and other school officials training in how to keep peace in classrooms and in hallways. It may be helpful for teachers to be able to spot trouble before violence breaks out and to have support services in place when needed. "Too many teachers come unprepared to deal with it all," says NSSC director Ron Stephens. "Like the teacher who told me, 'I got my training the day the kid pointed a gun at my face.' "

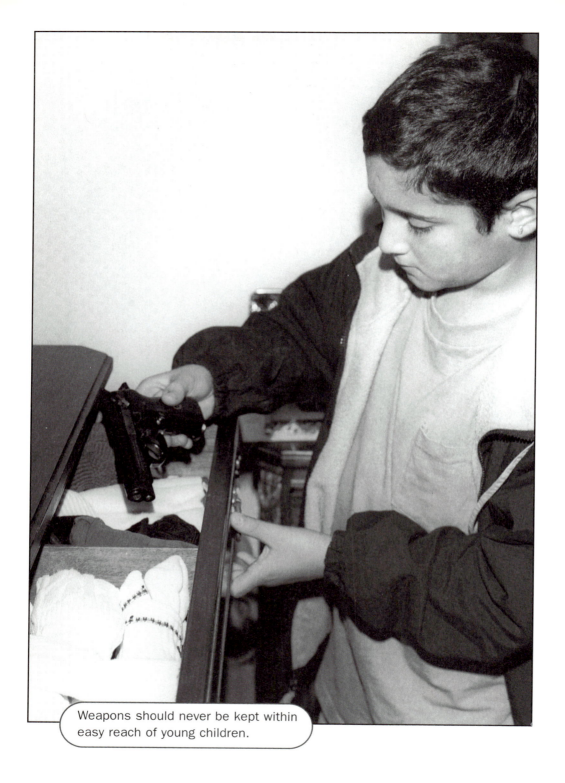

Weapons should never be kept within easy reach of young children.

Chapter Seven

What You Can Do

Adults are working hard to end the problem of weapons in school and at home. But all the parents, police, school officials, lawmakers, and other adults put together don't have as much power as teens themselves to solve this problem. Here are some things you can do.

At Home

1. Stay away from guns and other weapons.

2. Keep sisters and brothers—especially younger ones—away from all weapons.

3. Talk with your parents about whether weapons are really needed at home. Remind them that there are risks, especially if:

   • There are small children in the house.

- There is anyone very excitable or who has talked of suicide.

- Your parents are untrained in the handling of weapons.

4. If the decision is to keep weapons in the house, ask your parents to follow these safety rules:

- Store the weapons in a locked case, cabinet, or closet. The harder the storage area is to break into, the better. A locked closet or wooden cabinet is better than a locked glass display case.

- Store weapons unloaded and uncocked—be sure to check if there's a round left inside the gun. It's often the case that one bullet is in the firing chamber even when the bullet-holding unit (magazine) has been taken out.

- Store bullets in a separate, locked case or container away from the weapon.

- Put a padlock, trigger lock, or other safety device on the weapon itself. These are sold in gun shops or sporting goods stores. Don't depend only on the gun's "safety" lever.

- Never hide a gun or other weapon in a bedside drawer or under a mattress or pillow. These locations are sure to be checked out if a prowler breaks in, and they are also much too easy for children to get at!

- Do not store a weapon along with valuables, such as cash or jewelry. Burglars often get their guns this way.

- Learn proper gun care and cleaning. Adults should be alone and in a safe place when cleaning a gun. Before cleaning, they should check the weapon twice to be sure it's unloaded.

- Have anyone old enough to handle a weapon attend a firearms safety class. These are offered by gun clubs, camps, and some school systems and police groups.

- Treat other weapons, such as knives and bows and arrows, with similar care and caution.

5. If you know that someone is mishandling a weapon, get away from the scene and tell an adult as soon as possible. If there is an accident involving a weapon, dial 911 and tell the operator that there is a police or medical emergency.

In School

1. Remember that there is no good reason to have a weapon with you in school. Never bring one to school.

2. Tell your friends that you are against weapons in school.

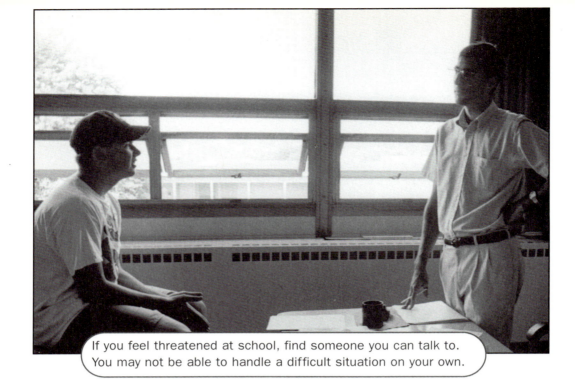

If you feel threatened at school, find someone you can talk to. You may not be able to handle a difficult situation on your own.

3. If you see or know someone who has a weapon, don't let him or her think you are impressed. Tell a teacher or other adult, either openly or by placing a note in the person's mailbox. (You don't have to give your name.) Even though your classmate may get in trouble, you may be doing him or her, as well as others, a big favor.

4. If you are threatened with a weapon, don't try to fight back. Give the person whatever he or she wants and report it to the authorities right away.

For Yourself

If you feel the need to pack a weapon, listen to the message from a young man named Chris Hans. Hans was interviewed on an ABC-TV news show.

Hans, a fourteen-year-old, straight-A student in a good school, began to carry weapons when he started having problems with his parents and teachers. He didn't feel he could tell anyone about these problems. But with a gun or a knife in his possession, Chris felt powerful, in charge.

One day, Chris was especially upset and confused. He didn't think about asking for help. He didn't know anyone would be willing to listen to what he had to say. Instead, he decided to use the power he carried in his pocket. He walked into his school with a loaded gun and knocked on a teacher's door. When the unsuspecting teacher opened it, Chris shot her to death. Then he shot the vice principal, injuring him seriously. Chris was arrested, tried, convicted, and sent to jail.

Since the shootings, Chris Hans has had a lot of time to think about what he did—and he'll have a lot more. His sentence is 230 years behind bars!

The reporter asked Chris what advice he had for other youngsters who might also be tempted to use weapons to solve their problems.

"Tell someone how you feel," said Chris, "and if that person won't listen, tell someone else, and then someone else. Find someone who will listen. Because if you don't, things will get a lot worse, real quick."

Glossary

action toys Group of toys that includes guns and other weapons, usually marketed to young boys.

assault Physical attack on someone.

debate Discussion of a question or issue. Arguments for and against are given in turn.

firearm Rifle, shotgun, or handgun.

gun control The idea that private ownership of guns should be more regulated by law. Under most proposed plans, the private ownership of handguns would be banned and rifle ownership would be more tightly controlled.

handgun Pistol or revolver.

martial arts Methods of fighting that use the hands and feet as weapons, developed by the Chinese, Japanese, Koreans, and other Far Eastern peoples. Karate is one form.

metal detector Machine that uses magnets to sound an alarm when there is a metal object present. Detectors are made in both walk-through and hand-held units.

Oriental stars Sharply pointed, star-shaped blades.

Oriental sticks Martial arts weapon made up of two sticks connected by a short chain.

pros and cons Arguments for and against an issue.

Right to Bear Arms Section of the United States Constitution that ensures the right of all citizens to have guns to defend their freedom.

suicide Taking one's own life.

switchblade Specially made pocketknife that can be opened very quickly, using only one hand.

weapon Gun, knife, or any other item used to cause harm or damage.

Where to Go for Help

In the United States

Center to Prevent Handgun Violence
1225 Eye Street NW, Suite 1100
Washington, DC 20005
(202) 898-0792

Coalition to Stop Gun Violence
1000 16th Street NW, Suite 603
Washington, DC 20036
(202) 530-0340
Web site: http://www.csgv.org

National School Safety Center
141 Duesenberg Drive, Suite 11
Westlake Village, CA 91362
(805) 373-9977
Web site: http://www.nssc1.org

In Canada

National Clearinghouse on Family Violence
1907 D1 Jeanne Mance Building, Tunney's Pasture
Ottawa, ON K1A 1B4
(800) 267-1291

For Further Reading

Hamburg, Beatrix. *Violence in America's Classes*. New York: Cambridge University Press, 1998.

Imbimbo, T. "Playing It Cool: Violence Prevention for Adolescents." *Seventeen*, February 1990, p. 40.

Katz, L. G. "How TV Violence Affects Kids." *Parents*, January 1991, p. 113.

Kreiner, Anna. *Everything You Need to Know About School Violence*. New York: Rosen Publishing Group, 1996.

Lacayo, Richard. "Under Fire." *Time*, January 29, 1990, pp. 16–23.

Landau, Elaine. *Teenage Violence*. Englewood Cliffs, NJ: Julian Messner, 1990.

Margolis, Jeffrey. *Everything You Need to Know About Teens Who Kill*. New York: Rosen Publishing Group, 2000.

Sickmund, Melissa, Howard N. Snyder, and Eileen Poe-Yamagata. *Juvenile Offenders and Victims: 1997 Update on Violence*. Washington, DC: Office of Juvenile Justice and Delinquency Prevention, 1997.

Woods, Geraldine. *The Right to Bear Arms*. New York: Franklin Watts, 1986.

Index

About the Author

A native of New York City and graduate of City College of New York, Jay Schleifer taught for five years in the New York school system with an emphasis on special education. He was editor of *Know Your World*, a high/low publication, for five years, and has authored more than twenty high/low books on a variety of topics. Jay now works as a publishing company executive and lives in the Midwest.

Photo Credits

Cover photo by Dick Smolinski.
P. 2 © AP/Worldwide; p. 9 © Douglas Burrow/Gamma Liaison; p. 12 by Mike Okoniewski; p. 17 Archive Photos; pp. 20, 22, 30, 49 © Paul Howell/Gamma Liaison; p. 27 © Gary Kanadjian/AP/Worldwide; p. 40 © Corbis International; p. 43 © Gary Stewart/AP/Worldwide; p. 46 © Terry Ashe/Gamma Liaison; p. 52 by Stuart Rabinowitz; p. 56 by Mary Lauzon.